GW00771298

Celebration

The Christmas Cat Book

Merry Christmas

Norcross, New York

To:

From:

Celebration: THE CHRISTMAS CAT BOOK

©2006 Margaret Denk

ISBN: 1933-176-07-5
Published by Red Rock Press
New York, New York U.S.A.

www.RedRockPress.com

All images in this book come from antique Christmas cards collected by Margaret Denk for Red Rock Press. Attributions have been made to the best of our knowledge. If we have erred in any identification, please notify Red Rock Press by post or email: Rights@RedRockPress.com, and corrections will be made in any subsequent editions of the book.

Library of Congress Cataloging-in-Publication Data

Denk, Margaret.
  Celebration : the Christmas cat book / by Margaret Denk.
    p. cm.
  ISBN 1-933176-07-5
1. Christmas cards. 2. Cats in art. I. Title.

NC1866.C5D46 2006
741.6'84—dc22
                      2006005536
Printed in Singapore

to

Natalie Stephenson
a great cat lover

Celebration

The Christmas Cat Book

Margaret Denk

Red Rock Press
New York, New York

With best Christmas Wishes

Introduction

People have admired and even worshipped cats for eons but we have not always lived cozily with them.

It is the feline who usually decides where he or she would like to be. Until a couple of hundred years ago, most domesticated cats preferred to keep their distance from those deluded enough to think of themselves as their owners.

These proud cats were pleased to work for independent livings, patrolling fields, barns, storage sheds and sometimes the attics, cellars and kitchens of homes, grand or humble. They protected human foodstuffs by going after mice and thieving insects.

This is not to say that the mistress or children of the house never stroked a kitten and beamed at its answering purr. But despite gestures of affection, mutual respect allowed cats to curl up on their own home spots.

It was not until the 1800s that many people started making their favorite animals into *pets,* bribing them with dishes of cream and cajoling them to the hearth. Above all, the Victorians were sentimentalists. No sooner, it seems, was a charming cat in the drawing room than its mistress or master attributed to it all manner of human characteristics. Household cats were part of the family and so became an emblem of their Christmas celebrations.

Felis catus became a model for Christmas tree ornaments and, especially for holiday cards. The cat's popularity as a pet soared just about the time the exchange of seasonal cards became a custom in England, the United States and elsewhere. The first known printed Christmas cards date from 1843. Handmade individual cards preceded this and cats may have appeared on some.

Christmas cats had particular appeal to children. From a dark year of the U.S. Civil War, there is a lighthearted account, written by an 11 year-old girl, of a Christmas celebration at the home of Confederacy President Jefferson Davis. She noted with delight that Davis gave cotton-stuffed toy cats as gifts to his younger guests.

In this collection, there is a Christmas cat card created 40 years later in London that an even younger child gave to a special kitten.

Some feline fanciers, on both sides of the Atlantic, became devoted to developing cat breeds, with roots that were either local or as distant as Asia. The first official cat show was held in 1871 at London's Crystal Palace.

Raphael Tuck & Sons, Christmas card maker to Queen Victoria, preferred to use more common cats in dozens of the hundreds of cards he and his sons produced for royals, and for commoners.

Although most of Tuck's lovely holiday cats were painted in naturalistic poses, his firm also released witty, anthropomorphic illustrations of Christmas cats and a few cards featuring black and white photos of kittens.

The British engravers, Hildesheimer & Faulkner, also produced cards with adorable Christmas cat images. Some of their cards featured cats in human rather than feline activity.

Christmas games with cat names were popular. Some holiday games, such as Blind Man's Bluff, which stars in a Charles Dickens description of a Christmas party, go back hundreds and hundreds of years. These games, beloved by Victorians, were played by people of all ages.

One such game, The Minister's Cat, is a word game that came to be played at Christmas fetes in Canada. The person beginning the game must use an "A" word, starting, for example, by saying, "The minister's cat is an *amusing* cat." The next person, who adds a "B" word, might go on to say, "The minister's cat is *beautiful* and *amusing*."

By the early 20th century, Bavaria had become a center of Christmas-card printing, producing holiday postcards, some with sentiments in English or French or Russian. English and American card publishers used both domestic and German print-ers. Christmas cats were popular many places.

To this day, illustrators draw Christmas cats to deliver holiday wishes and good cheer. But the antique cards are really special. I hope this collection of them will delight cat lovers for many Christmases to come.

—Margaret Denk
Chicago

14

Table of Contents

A Joyous Christmastide

Chapter One

Cozy Christmas Cats

"No house is a home without a cat." This was near to a late-Victorian cliché.

In many a country home, the cat could be found on the sunny window seat in the morning or curled in front of the fire on a cold afternoon while the family's dogs still spent most of their time in the kennel. Many city dwellers must have decided it was both more useful (remember the city mouse) and easier (no walks required) to have a cat than a dog.

Christmas Greetings

A Merry Christmas

19

Not all cats, however, were allowed upstairs at night. It took the mid-20th century invention of kitty litter to secure the indoor status of pet kittens and cats.

In most other ways, however, the late Victorian period was the cat's meow.

To Wish you a merry Christmas and a bright New Year

Christmas Greetings

Travelling Persians.

Merry Christmas and

Happy New Year!

J. OTTMANN LITH. CO. N.Y.

Loving Christmas Greetings

Welcome to the happy Day
Of love and mirth and fun
and play -
I'm hoping it may hold for you
Many pleasures sweet and new
I send my love and wish that all
That's glad and bright to you befall.

23

May You Have A Merry Christmas

To wish you Happiness

The first successful women's magazine, *Godey's Lady's Book,* tried, in the 1870s, to debunk a myth (which still has some force) that owning a cat marked a woman as without romantic prospects. "It is settled now that cats and spinsterhood have no connection," a Godey's writer proclaimed.

A Merry Christmas

I hope, since Christmas
Last was here,
You've had
Twelve months
of
Joy
and
Cheer.

A Merry Christmas.

An article published in the New Year's Eve 1881 edition of *Harper's Illustrated* announced that the year had come in which American Christmas cards outshone imported specimens. Among *Harper's* favorites of the year, were small cards with amusing cat images.

With hearty Christmas Wishes

Early Christmas cards are a trove of cute cats. Only rarely is a cat pictured with a woman who appears elderly. Both before and after the turn of the 19th-to-20th century, a beautiful young woman in holiday best might be pictured with a winsome kitten. More frequently, cats were painted in the company of happy children at Christmastime.

A Happy Xmas

Under the Mistletoe

With best Christmas Wishes

But most often, beautiful kittens appear on their own in Christmas settings—at the center of a wreath, framed by red berries, or in a holiday-decorated basket. Even when no humans are in the picture, the image is implicitly a domestic one, full of the warmth and happiness that perhaps only a contented cat can signify.

The British greeting-card masters, Raphael Tuck & Sons produced the sweet Christmas cat in the basket that you can find here. Note that this Tuck cat is blue-eyed and dark grey, not the coal black of many good-luck black cats featured in the next chapter.

Bonne Année

With every Good Wish for a Joyful Christmas!

35

A Merry Christmas.

The card's greeting, *Bonne Année,* is, of course, "Happy New Year" in French. The Tuck firm eventually printed cards in Paris (and New York) as well as London. Many early holiday cards, especially those starring black cats, were geared toward New Year. Our next chapter will look more closely at that.

Another particularly notable card is the small one on the facing page. Here a white kitten, at home in a white satin shoe, gazes at two other items of feminine luxury, a soft pink scarf and gold medallion necklace.

WITH KINDEST GREETINGS FOR THIS CHRISTMAS DAY.

HM
S. Hildesheimer & Co.

No 75. Copyright

A Merry Christmas

Dec. 25 - 1910

Another personal favorite, probably because it's a bit unusual, features two impish cats gazing at a snowman with a cigar smacked between his lips. On Christmas Day, 1910, a mother gave this card, made in Germany, to her son, Master Howard Gibson of Woodstock, Vermont. Did Howard live apart from his "mama" who signed the card? We cannot know. But we may assume that they were together that long ago Christmas as the card has not a street address or, more tellingly, a stamp.

Chapter Two

'Tis the Season of
Good-Luck Black Cats

The eighteenth-century poet, Christopher Smart, wrote that his cat, Jeffrey "counteracts the Devil who is Death by brisking about his life."

Like many a seer ahead of his time, Christopher passed his final days in a madhouse. But Smart was, well, smart: he saw that the essence of "cathood" has nothing to do with evil. Cats embody *life*. And if they enjoy nine lives—often surviving what would kill lesser species—it's because they are extremely well-balanced and just plain lucky.

SER. 138

A merry Christmas!

For Christmas is a Merry Time!

43

GOOD LUCK

With all Kind
Christmas Thoughts.

Christmas Wishes

The linkage between witchcraft and black cats goes back centuries. Black cats were mixed up in magic; black cats had a line to the supernatural.

The Enlightenment didn't wipe out superstition. To this day, there are those who shudder when a black cat crosses their path. But for the love of cats, many Victorians cast away dark ideas about black cats while still retaining the notion that such pets had a special connection to luck: black cats signified good fortune.

It's no small matter that Britain's most significant rags-to-riches legend revolves around Dick Whittington, the tattered young seafarer whose single possession, a rat-devouring cat, turns out to be of surpassing value. The cat who made Dick rich remains a hero of English Christmas pantomimes. The moral is: cats bring great, good luck.

Tales of Me and Ma

will
bring
you

Good
Luck

and a Merry

CHRISTMAS

From

C-77
©△

47

Good Fortune
attend you!

CHRISTMAS
GREETINGS

and all
Good Wishes
for a happy
New Year

49

FAIR
THOUGHTS
AND
HAPPY
HOURS
BE
THINE.

A MERRY XMAS To YOU.

50

Sending holiday greeting cards is a habit that became seeded in England and North America in the second half of the nineteenth century. The sending of cards arose as a response to the scattering of family and friends as the British came to reside in the far corners of empire, and as Americans pushed too far west to travel back east to home for Christmas and New Year. Many had also left their home provinces to flock to large cities and mill towns.

A good number of the early holiday cards posted to family members and friends mentioned both Christmas and New Year.

When the calendar opens on January first, twelve un-played months lie ahead. A hundred years and longer ago, it would have been thought odd to welcome the year with a squalling baby— what trouble is *that*? Instead, one conveyed one's top wishes for a lucky new year with the potent good-fortune luck symbol: the black cat.

By the early 20th century, the good-luck black cat presided over Christmas cards even when wishes for the coming year were not part of a card's message.

> Just a word in your ear,
> 'Tis the time of year,
> When the warmth of kind wishes makes all hearts to glow.
> So I send you this cat —
> I am very fond of that,
> For a black cat is always the luckiest you know.

A HAPPY CHRISTMAS.

Just a word in your ear,
'Tis the time of the year,
When the warmth of kind wishes makes all hearts to glow,
So I send you this cat –
I am very fond of that,
For a black one is always the luckiest, you know.

53

Série 4. 11.

Chapter Three

Almost Human
Christmas Cats

Some might argue that cats shed their natural dignity once they agreed to move in with slovenly, often noisy people.

But anyone who has lived with a cat is likely to attest that while the occasional kitten might seem a bit deficient in the natural-reserve department, adult cats invariably know how to keep their distance when they so choose.

Elephants have played butlers and other servants in certain (admittedly quite hilarious) circus skits; horses and dogs may

Hearty Christmas Wishes

perform in foolish costumes, but pray, when was the last time you saw a cat dance to someone else's tune?

The truth is that cats have managed to keep their *amour propre,* their innate self esteem, in almost all circumstances. But

A Merry Christmas

that hasn't stopped some illustrators, even talented ones, from ridiculously depicting cats and kittens on Christmas cards.

How ridiculous? Cats have been rendered anthropomorphically, i.e. they have been placed in human clothes and/or postures and have been shown doing the kind of comic things that some humans enjoy.

I don't need to tell you that no cat has ever actually *posed* for such a painting or drawing. Rather the artist has sketched from his or her own violently cute imagination.

Still, we love the merry-making kitties who've become part of the Christmas cat tradition. They make us smile.

Who could resist the image on this page—four cool cats (look at their faces!) in nightcaps patiently standing on their hind legs as

they survey presents and a gift-filled pair of boots. Also on the hearth is a very *domestic* mouse family. (What else could a mouse in an apron convey?) The painter of this scene was either Raphael Tuck, one of his sons or someone in their employ.

That postcard was never mailed because its intended recipient lived under the same roof as its "sender." That sender was a young child (the writing on the card makes that clear). The child addressed the card to: "my kitten."

In this collection, you'll also meet a pretty Victorian milk-maid cat, two blue-coated kittens approaching their bespectacled mother's door, and a rather electric-looking cat enjoying a Christmas letter with his morning milk.

Fine Christmas cats, one and all.

A joyous Christmas.

A MERRY
CHRISTMAS